™

BATMAN

IN *Detective* COMICS

FEATURING THE COMPLETE COVERS OF THE FIRST 25 YEARS

ABBEVILLE PRESS · PUBLISHERS

NEW YORK · LONDON · PARIS

Batman created by Bob Kane.

Tiny Folio and the Abbeville logo are trademarks of Abbeville Press, Inc.

Many of the covers reproduced in this volume were provided from the private collections of Craig Delich, Joe Desris, Ron Killian, and Mike Tiefenbacher. All cover credits researched and assembled by Joe Desris.

The captions note the pencil artists, followed by the ink artists, for each cover as could best be determined; however, as it was not standard practice to credit artists in the comic-book industry until the last few decades, this list may not be definitive. While the authors have endeavored to identify all of the artists involved, they apologize to any person misidentified or not identified and invite such person to inform them of the error.

First edition

Library of Congress Cataloging-in-Publication Data

Batman in detective comics : featuring the complete covers of the first 25 years.
     p. cm.
    Includes index.
    ISBN 1-55859-643-7
    1. Batman (Comic strip) 2. Comic book covers—United States.
PN6728.B36B4 1993
741.5'973—dc20

93-2276
CIP

INTRODUCTION
by Joe Desris

When you're looking for something to read, what's the first thing you notice? Consider your own decision in purchasing this book. The most important element of any magazine or book is its cover. Without an exciting exterior to grab the reader's attention, how can strong sales be guaranteed?

As the late Sol Harrison, former Production Manager of DC Comics, once observed: "The covers are our showcase. They are dealt with differently from the insides. They are printed on special coated paper, printed on better presses, and for these reasons will show every line so much clearer. Color is very important."

This was not only true at a 1959 staff meeting where Harrison—later president of DC Comics—made these remarks, but it remains true today and certainly was valid when the first issue of *Detective Comics* hit the newsstands in early 1937. "The purpose of the cover, I think," observes *Detective Comics*'s first editor, Vincent Sullivan, "was just simply to have the person pay for it and pick it up. It may not have had [any] connection with the stories inside."

With gun-toting cops and robbers of early issues offering a taste of the detective story content, such covers were designed more to sell comics than highlight any particular story. Although Batman's successful introduction made clear which story to feature, roughly the first half of the covers in this book still interpret content allegorically rather than literally (and sometimes not at all!). Even the fantastic cover exploits of the Caped Crusader were often irrelevant to the interiors. Indeed, The Joker's first Detective Comics appearance in cover 45 is unheralded, as are Penguin's introductory adventures (covers 58, 59), while cover 40 features The Joker but has a different villain in the story. Of course, not all great events went without fanfare. In time, as DC modified editorial and production approaches regarding color, copy, and design, covers featured specific content. Prime examples are the first appearances of Robin (cover 38), Riddler (cover 140), Batwoman (cover 233), and Bat-Mite (cover 267), as well as origins of the Batcave (cover 205) and the famous costume (cover 235).

Decades later, the book became essentially a Batman comic with a different title, although it began as a detective anthology with brand-new material—still a relatively novel idea in 1937. Contents included Fred Guardineer's Speed Saunders and Jerry Siegel and Joe Shuster's Spy and Slam Bradley, as well as later appearances by Jim Chambers's Crimson Avenger, and others such as Larry Steele and Fu Manchu. One day, editor Vincent Sullivan mentioned to cartoonist Bob Kane that he should develop a new super-hero-type character. The result: Batman. The Gotham Guardian's first appearance (cover 27) and meteoric success quickly led to his usurping regular cover position as of cover 35. Kane's humor submissions (Oscar the Gumshoe, Spanky and Cranky, Jest A Second) also appeared in *Detective* before a successful Caped Crusader completely consumed Kane's time.

Although editor of the series until early 1940, Sullivan also pencilled, inked, and produced a color guide for the first issue's cover.

"I don't know why I didn't assign it to somebody else," he recalls. "But I did it. I was not what you would call an illustrator; I was a cartoonist. In other words, that is not my forte; mine is comic characters but I could occasionally do something like that. The reason I did this Oriental figure is that I had been a reader of Sax Rohmer's books [about] Fu Manchu. I think I must have either had an illustration from the *Saturday Evening Post* or *Colliers* or one of those magazines. I was influenced by the illustration that appeared in connection with the Sax Rohmer stories."

Following Sullivan's pencils and inks of Chin Lung for cover 1, Creig Flessel became regular cover artist for the subsequent eighteen issues. "Why did I do the covers?" Flessel asks rhetorically of his Depression-era work. "Because I sat there. I was smart enough to put a drawing board in there and I realized that money was going to be scarce, and so I'd get my money every week. [Editor] Whit Ellsworth would say, 'Fless, we need a cover,' and you'd just do a cover." Flessel pencilled, inked, and made up a color guide for his work.

His actual first effort for *Detective* depicted a yellow ghoul wearing a bright red cloak and holding a bloody dagger. Although his art made it to the proofing stage, what could have become the medium's first horror cover was ultimately rejected.

"There were several that I didn't sign," recalls Flessel. "I don't know why. I just didn't get my name on it, that's all." Dr. Fu Manchu's appearance on cover 18 is one example. "I think that was Leo O'Mealia's character," Flessel adds, "and I think I sort of felt, well, I'm doing the thing and Leo isn't around so I won't sign it because it wasn't mine. I was being altruistic."

Another unsigned Flessel treatment is cover 34. "The *Corinthia* is the name of the boat we took our vacation on," he says, "and it sunk during the war—the first boat to be sunk by a German submarine. It went down in the English Channel. If you look in the files, you can find a picture of it turning turtle and hundreds of people climbing like ants."

Artist Fred Guardineer frequently signed his work. While illustrating Speed Saunders stories inside *Detective Comics*, he simultaneously pencilled and inked seven covers. He also produced several covers for *Action Comics* and *Adventure Comics* during the same period.

Cover signing was commonplace on DC's 1930s comics but the practice faded in the early 1940s. With six exceptions, even Bob Kane's ubiquitous endorsement vanished after cover 57 (dated 1941). As Batman's popularity demanded more material, it became increasingly difficult for one individual to keep up the pace. Kane's signature after cover 37 more frequently reflects pencilling rather than finished art, as Jerry Robinson and George Roussos gradually took over more of the chores. Fred Ray's pencilled layouts with Robinson's additional pencilling and inks for cover 58 mark the first Batman cover devoid of Kane's hand. Kane's work on cover 82 was his last in a regular sequence. From late 1943 until late 1946, he essentially stopped pencilling comic-book stories and covers to work on the syndicated Batman newspaper strip; however, his work can be seen again on cover 95 and several later issues.

According to these covers, an apparent abundance of home-front crime during World War II kept Batman stuck in Gotham City.

Unlike Superman, the Caped Crusader evidently lacked the necessary superpowers to resolve such global conflicts. Yet the war crept into all aspects of life (covers 78, 101), while interior stories such as "Blitzkrieg Bandits!" (*Batman* cover 21, February–March 1944) were more direct in handling topical matters.

A backup feature, the Boy Commandos, was introduced in *Detective Comics* issue 65 and featured on the front cover. "Most of the time," recalls artist Joe Simon, referring to his collaboration with Jack Kirby on the Commandos, "I would do layouts, Jack would pencil them, then I would ink them. We wouldn't have let anyone else do the cover." In this instance, to make the Gotham Guardians appear more like they typically did, Robinson inked the Batman figure and at least partially inked Robin.

Originally working outside of the DC offices, Kane, Robinson, and Roussos essentially had free rein on cover design. While other artists later collaborated with DC editors, the trio did not have to submit cover concepts or rough sketches for advance editorial approval. This continued even when Robinson and Roussos were brought into the DC bullpen late in 1940 and put on salary. "We never showed them the covers before we went in," recalls Robinson, "and it just continued afterwards."

A string of Jerry Robinson's realistic, posterlike exteriors (covers 67–72) are from a significant period when he completely illustrated a number of covers and stories independently of Bob Kane and George Roussos. Note that Jack Burnley had pencilled and inked Batman and Robin figures on the cover of *New York World's Fair* (1940), and a Burnley Batman story in *Detective Comics* issue 65 beat Robinson's first fully solo story to the newsstands by one month (*Batman* issue 12, August–September 1942); although Dick Sprang's largely independent work was initiated in 1941, it still remained unpublished at this point. Ever since George Roussos was hired in May 1940, published Batman material had been a collaborative effort between Kane, Robinson, and Roussos. But this large group of solo Robinson efforts was a significant and lengthy departure from the norm, and they paved the way for more of the same. This variety of artists soon became standard practice as cover 84 kicked off a series of ten covers by Sprang.

It was editor Whitney Ellsworth who allowed Robinson to illustrate Batman stories completely on his own. Jack Schiff and Mort Weisinger "were really story editors," Robinson remembers, "whereas Whit was the top editor, and also being the cartoonist of the group, acted as art director. We were all in one room. It was a big thing when Whit moved into his own office. Before that, he was three feet away. I was responsible to Whit and I would say, 'I'd like to do this story or this cover.' I think he was kind of a mentor when I was there. I was so young and he gave me the responsibility of doing important stuff at the time. I assume he must have liked the work I was doing; appreciated it. I remember I had a very easy relationship with him.

"I colored a number of stories that I had time for," Robinson continues, "or that I particularly liked doing, but I didn't do a lot." Coloring was usually the domain of Raymond Perry, former head colorist at DC for many years, and the man who colored the majority of covers in this volume.

Other artists typically received direction on cover assignments from Ellsworth, Schiff, or Weisinger. "I worked directly with Ellsworth and whatever they would send me, I'd do," says Jack Burnley, recalling his Batman- and Superman-related covers. "All those covers I did were Ellsworth's ideas; every one of them. If I had wanted to think up covers, I'm sure he would have been glad to have me do it, but I wasn't interested in that." Burnley received a sketch on butcher paper in very rough dummy style. "[But] essentially it was right there. *The Justice Society* was handled by Shelly Mayer. He would also rough out covers. He was a cartoonist himself. I did a couple of *All Star* covers, and I'm sure that Mayer roughed them out because they certainly weren't my ideas." While at DC, Burnley also illustrated covers for *World's Finest Comics, Batman, Adventure Comics* (he did create original concepts for his Starman covers), *Action Comics, Superman, Star-Spangled Comics,* and the 1940 edition of *New York World's Fair.*

Burnley, who also worked on the syndicated Batman newspaper strip, adds, "Sometimes I would take too long on the Sundays and they'd complain. They'd want me to do more than just pencil a Sunday [strip]. So they'd usually throw in a couple of covers or something."

Dick Sprang was initially hired to illustrate Batman stories in 1941. His work was intentionally committed to inventory and left unpublished, largely due to concerns about Bob Kane being drafted into World War II. Sprang later began receiving cover assignments and ultimately pencilled and inked thirty-two of the covers reprinted here. His first published cover of Batman appeared on *Batman* cover 19 (October–November 1943).

Alert comic-art aficionados may notice that Sprang's quality seems to vary. Contrast the polished cover 87 with the labored 88. This is partially due to Sprang's earliest work being intermingled with more current submissions. In addition, the art for covers 84 and 88 is probably among his earliest cover assignments, developed after drawing the characters for only a short time. Sprang's style quickly became slicker and more polished, and more of his own interpretations came through as he moved away from a handful of early story layouts by Ed Kressy and initial editorial directions to emulate the Batman house style of Kane and Robinson. "At one time," remarks Sprang, "I know it was suggested to copy Robinson. Finally, Whit told me, 'Do anything you want with Batman. Just go your way.' Well, I considered that from many angles. I decided that the essential figure should be kept as it was but I'd thicken his waist somewhat. Make him a little more athletic and fluid than Kane did, although Robinson made him very fluid. Shortened his ears a little bit and so on. And that was it.

"Sometimes in the office, we'd discuss a cover," Sprang continues. "Most of the time, Whit would tell me, 'I need a cover; any kind of a Batman cover.' I'd just go home and dream up something with no relationship to anything in the story. You remember the canoe about to go over the waterfall [cover 100]? At that time, I was studying the history and the construction of birch bark canoes. So that was in my mind. I dreamed up this thing going over the waterfall. Whit, bless his heart, he'd give me carte blanche on this stuff. I don't know what the reader thought."

"I got a lot more [cover assignments] when I lived in New York than I did when I moved to Arizona," says Sprang, "although I did quite a few out here, as the dates will confirm." He not only received written directions from Ellsworth but from Schiff and Weisinger as well. After moving out west in 1946, Sprang was mailed sketches and notes for developing covers. For example, Mort Weisinger sent him these instructions, dated December 2, 1948, regarding issue 147: "The cover should show Tiger Shark (wearing his helmet) and one of his thugs standing on the ocean, wearing their air-inflated skates. I think the size of the skates should be exagerrated [*sic*] thruout [*sic*] the story, so as to make a good, provocative picture. The two villains are firing with automatic pistols at Batman & Robin, who are overhead, clinging to the ladder of the Batplane, which is hovering over the scene. You needn't show all of the Batplane, as the point is to show B & R as prominently as possible in the picture. Natch, they are at bay, what with the leaden slugs whistling past them. I think the villains should be on the right side of the cover, B & R on the left. Please leave room for a blurb in upper right hand corner. P.S. Please do the cover as fast as you can and send in airmail-special delivery." One can easily assess Sprang's contribution to the cover by contrasting these guidelines with the finished art of cover 147. Weisinger's comments about rushing the cover indicate how impending deadlines have apparently always been part of the publishing business.

The transitional postwar period saw more artists than ever before (or even during the next fifteen years) illustrating covers for *Detective Comics*. During the four years from issue 108 (1946) until a nearly uninterrupted stretch settled in with cover 157 (1950), Win Mortimer and Jim Mooney were newly hired while Ray Burnley returned from wartime duty. Charles Paris was now seen more frequently since his work on the syndicated Batman newspaper strip ended in 1946; he also pencilled a handful of stories, something unique to this time period for him. Dick Sprang's overall output dropped temporarily during his move, with more of his work again showing up near the end of this period (few covers would follow, although he drew numerous Batman stories). Jack Burnley's final efforts saw print (he departed in 1947), as did Bob Kane's last regular fully pencilled pages (Lew Sayre Schwartz became Kane's regular ghost in 1947). Jerry Robinson also departed, although his last work appeared in *Batman*. Additionally, Gene McDonald first inked interiors during this time (none of his material appeared on the covers of *Detective Comics*), while Stan Kaye's efforts on Batman interiors are also first seen at this point (he did ink a number of later covers).

The most prolific cover artist throughout these three hundred covers was Win Mortimer, who joined DC in 1945. His first cover effort for *Detective Comics* appeared on cover 110 (April 1946). Not only did he maintain a nearly unbroken string of forty-six issues (covers 169–214), he ultimately pencilled and inked eighty-seven of the covers reprinted in this book. Mortimer also did numerous covers for *Action Comics, Batman, Adventure Comics, World's Finest Comics,* and *Superman* during this time. "For the most part," he says, "Jack Schiff was the one that I was working with almost exclusively. Many times Mort Weisinger would have been the editor on the story stuff that I was doing, but covers always seemed to come from Jack Schiff. As I recall, I'd always pencil [some]thing and show it to him. There might be a change [but] more often [I'd] just go right ahead and do it."

From 1949 until 1956, Mortimer worked on the daily Superman syndicated newspaper strips at home, visiting the DC offices almost every week to drop off and pick up new material. "When I'd get in," he continues, "I would do whatever they'd throw at me; it was usually a cover, so it was almost like one a week. That's why the numbers pile up on these things." Mortimer left DC in 1956 to illustrate another daily newspaper strip, *David Crane*. He moved in and out of comics after the mid-1960s, again doing occasional work for DC over the years.

Issue 114 displays the first use of a smaller logo for *Detective Comics*. This version allowed more room for art, while further reductions (covers 150, 155) again improved the balancing of text and art.

Picking up or revising a splash page (the inside first page) to provide cover art was not a new idea, having been used on covers 76 and 78, but the process became a science beginning in 1947, being used on covers 124, 125, 129–31, 133, 135, 141, and 142. This not only saved the expense of commissioning a cover but more quickly pushed a book through production. Occasionally, missed deadlines or art lost in the mails may have necessitated such work.

Throughout the Batman's first twenty-seven years, the Riddler only appeared twice (covers 140, 142). It was not until *Batman* cover 171 (May 1965) and the success of the 1966 Batman TV series that the Prince of Puzzlers became a permanent fixture in Batman's rogues gallery.

Kay Kyser, a popular 1940s radio personality, appears on cover 144. Similar Hollywood efforts in other DC books cast Ann

Blyth, Ralph Edwards, and Orson Welles with Superman while Ozzie and Harriet, Alan Ladd, and Bob Hope earned their own comic book series.

The Batsignal from cover 150 is a reminder of one of Batman's most prominent modern features that is nowhere to be seen in this book: his black bat chest emblem set inside a yellow oval. Although not introduced until cover 327 (May 1964), the device is foreshadowed on occasion (covers 108, 150, 164, 171, 186, 196, 231, 233, 276).

In cover 156 a new Batmobile was introduced when the previous version was destroyed in a crash off a dynamited bridge. "That was a mechanical drawing," Sprang recalls of his work on the cover's blackboard. "I used compasses on that, everything."

The Joker wins as most frequent cover boy, his ghastly grin gracing eighteen issues (covers 40, 62, 69, 71, 76, 85, 91, 102, 109, 114, 118, 124, 128, 137, 149, 158, 180, 193). Technically, the Grim Jester appears on a total of twenty issues, although an explanation would give away secrets to stories not everyone may have read.

With rare exceptions, word balloons became standard practice on covers beginning with issue 176. This device had been used irregularly since first appearing in the series on cover 65.

From the beginning of *Detective Comics*, guns played an important part in depicting the role of criminals, serving to identify villains readily. The weapons became somewhat less frequent after cover 178 and uncommon after cover 235.

The Ajax Toy Co.'s Batplanes and Batmobiles on the cover of 197 would seem to imply the existence of such items in 1953; however, essentially no Batman toys had been licensed up to this point. Serious Batman merchandising began in 1966, due to the popularity of the TV series.

Sheldon Moldoff was Bob Kane's first ghost assistant on Batman (his background inking and lettering appeared in *Detective Comics* issues 30–35). From 1953 to 1967, Moldoff became Kane's full-time and longest-running ghost. Although 215 is technically his first cover, it was assembled from elements on the first and second pages of the story. Moldoff's first original cover work appears on 231.

The wash for cover 239 was the only occasion this unusual effect appeared on any Batman-related title. "It's the only one they were willing to take a chance on for some reason or other," recalls production man Jack Adler. Used more frequently on DC's war and science-fiction titles, wash covers presented a challenge. After the usual pencilling work, the cover could either be finished in pencils or a wash to provide levels of gray. "I had to instruct whoever was doing it," continues Adler. "It was a system that I worked out. Some of them took one shot at it and generally shied away. Some really were good at it but wouldn't want to do it because it was too time-consuming compared to line inking." For this particular effort, the wash was done by Adler himself. "Sol Harrison probably colored it," Adler concludes.

Curt Swan and Stan Kaye (also teaming up in *World's Finest Comics*) provided a realistic contrast to the cartoonier work of Moldoff. "I would go into the city to do the covers," Swan recalls of his trips to New York while freelancing for DC. "I did those in the art department. I would discuss covers with Mort Weisinger and work out what he wanted. He would have the idea and he would trust us to sketch it out, cover size, and come up with something that would parallel what his thinking was. I would rough it out full size and take it in to him, and he would request changes or say okay, proceed. That's the way it was done. And usually the inker was standing by, George Klein or Stan Kaye, whoever it happened to be at the time.

"[Style] was at the discretion of the editor," continues Swan. "They had what they felt was their model in mind, and usually it was the originator or the person that had been working on it previously. I was familiar with the character, though I didn't capture the Bob Kane flair. I wasn't able to absolutely ape the style of Bob Kane and inwardly, I didn't want to. So I had this conflict within myself. I didn't think it was that great, but he [Weisinger] liked my illustrative style. That's what I tried to achieve."

Regarding visualization of the pesty Bat-Mite from cover 267, Moldoff recalls, "I created the character from the script, but it was my original conception and all. The writer had come up with this little alien, the comic character from outer space that appears and disappears." Longtime Batman writer Bill Finger, a major player in defining Batman in his earliest adventures, was the story's author.

Some stories in *Batman* and *Detective Comics* stories provided source material for episodes of the 1966–68 *Batman* TV series. Catwoman's KittyCar ("The Funny Feline Felonies/The Joke's On Catwoman") had its foundations in the black roadster "kitty car" introduced in issue 122. The bank flood and a man slowly suffocating inside a metal tube puzzle from issue 140 made their way into "Batman's Anniversary/A Riddling Controversy." Egghead ("An

Egg Grows In Gotham/The Yegg Foes In Gotham") differed from issue 217's brainy Barney Barrows, though this story was likely the springboard for the character and provided the idea of a victim strapped into a question-and-answer machine used in the TV script. A statue-sculpting sequence with Mad Hatter originated in issue 230, appearing on TV as "The Thirteenth Hat/Batman Stands Pat," while other elements of issue 230 appear in "The Contaminated Cowl/The Mad Hatter Runs Afoul." The theft of various Egyptian relics in issue 253 provided a few plot threads to TV's "The Curse of Tut/The Pharaoh's in a Rut," although villainous King Tut was an original creation of the TV series.

Subject to fine tuning, this collection of covers shows how numerous successful bat-concepts, such as the utility belt, Robin, Alfred, the Batcave, and the Batmobile, have remained constant for over fifty years. Simultaneously, many interpretations can be seen in these covers, from lone vigilante (covers 27–37), to confounded crimefighter (cover 246), to campy space-traveling alien nemesis (cover 251), to heroic policeman (cover 46), to hapless doofus (cover 74), to admirable genius detective (cover 156).

Batman has evolved over the years, yet managed to remain the same. Perhaps it was this ability to change while retaining familiarity that made the material work. Such flexibility is certainly a tribute to the enduring creativity of Bob Kane, Bill Finger, and all their successors.

LIST OF ARTISTS

MARCH 1937; NO. 1
Cover artist: Vincent Sullivan

APRIL 1937; NO. 2
Cover artist: Creig Flessel

No. 3

MAY, 1937

Detective
COMICS

10¢

MAY 1937; NO. 3
Cover artist: Creig Flessel

JUNE 1937; NO. 4
Cover artist: Creig Flessel

JULY 1937; NO. 5
Cover artist: Creig Flessel

AUGUST 1937; NO. 6
Cover artist: Creig Flessel

SEPTEMBER 1937; NO. 7
Cover artist: Creig Flessel

OCTOBER 1937; NO. 8
Cover artist: Creig Flessel

NOVEMBER 1937; NO. 9
Cover artist: Creig Flessel

DECEMBER 1937; NO. 10
Cover artist: Creig Flessel

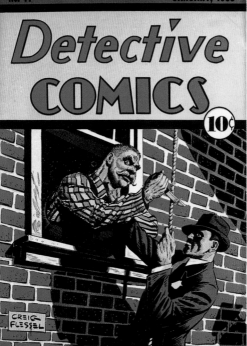

JANUARY 1938; NO. 11
Cover artist: Creig Flessel

MARCH 1938; NO. 13
Cover artist: Creig Flessel

MAY 1938; NO. 15
Cover artist: Creig Flessel

JUNE 1938; NO. 16
Cover artist: Creig Flessel

JULY 1938; NO. 17
Cover artist: Creig Flessel

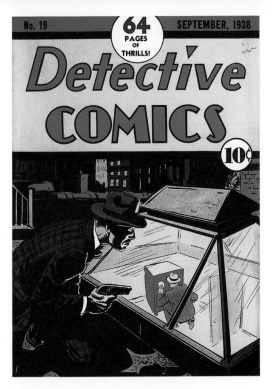

SEPTEMBER 1938; NO. 19
Cover artist: Creig Flessel

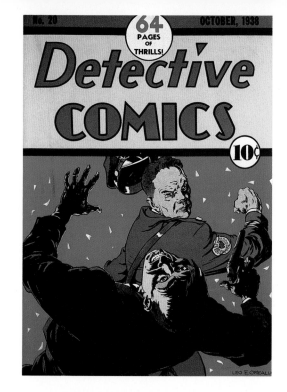

NOVEMBER 1938; NO. 21
Cover artist: Leo E. O'Mealia

JANUARY 1939; NO. 23
Cover artist: Fred Guardineer

FEBRUARY 1939; NO. 24
Cover artist: Fred Guardineer

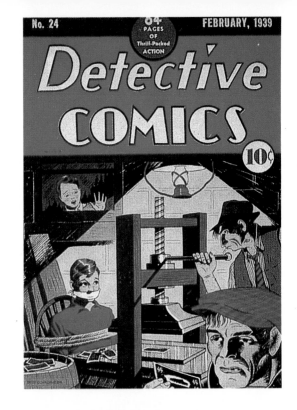

MARCH 1939; NO. 25
Cover artist: Fred Guardineer

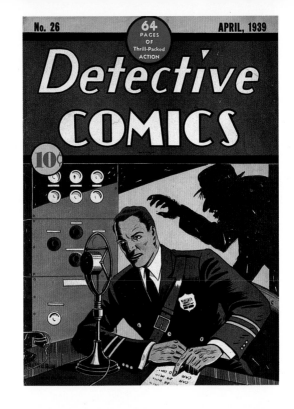

MAY 1939; NO. 27
Cover artist: Bob Kane

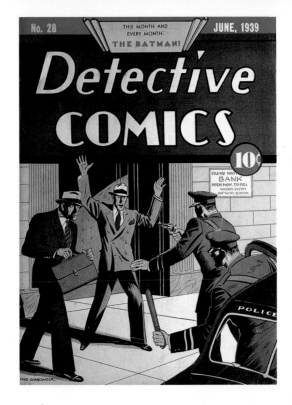

JULY 1939; NO. 29
Cover artist: Bob Kane

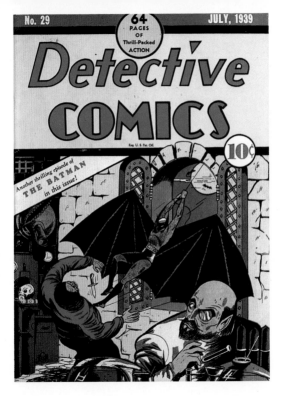

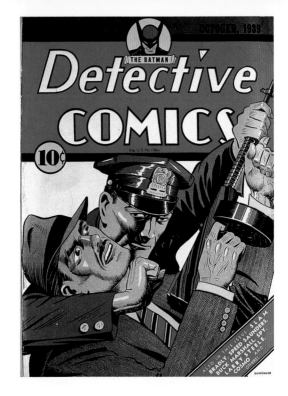

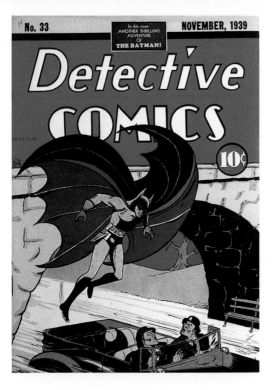

NOVEMBER 1939; NO. 33

Cover artist: Bob Kane

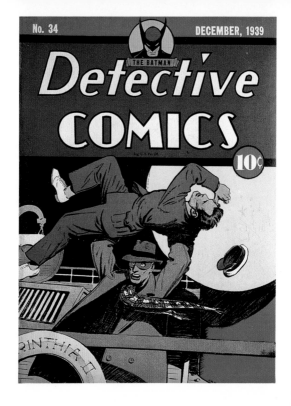

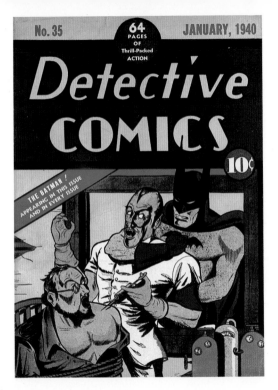

JANUARY 1940; NO. 35
Cover artist: Bob Kane

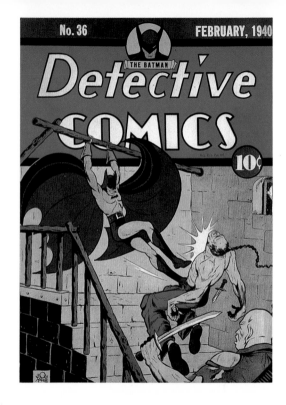

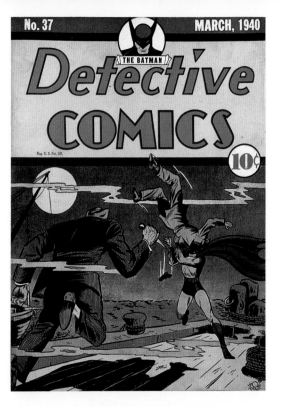

MARCH 1940; NO. 37
Cover artist: Bob Kane

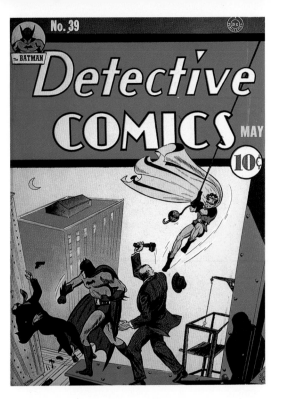

MAY 1940; NO. 39
Cover artists: Bob Kane, Jerry Robinson

JUNE 1940; NO. 40

Cover artists: Bob Kane, Jerry Robinson

JULY 1940; NO. 41
Cover artist: Bob Kane, Jerry Robinson

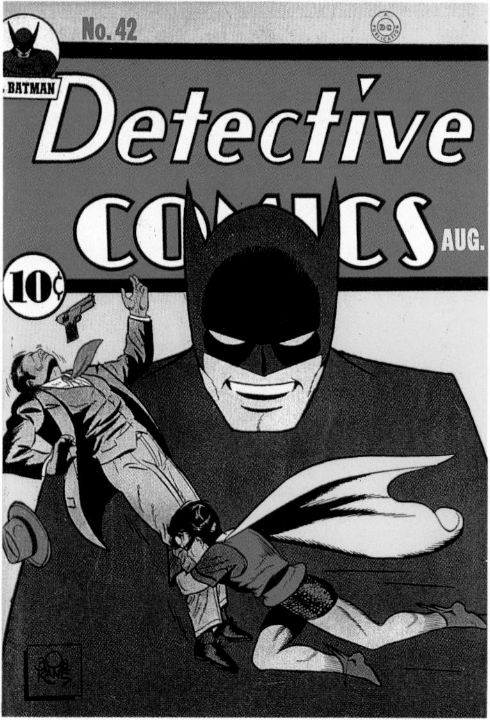

AUGUST 1940; NO. 42
Cover artists: Bob Kane, Jerry Robinson

SEPTEMBER 1940: NO. 43
Cover artists: Bob Kane, Jerry Robinson

OCTOBER 1940; NO. 44

Cover artists: Bob Kane, Jerry Robinson, George Roussos

NOVEMBER 1940; NO. 45
Cover artists: Bob Kane, Jerry Robinson, George Roussos

JANUARY 1941; NO. 47
Cover artists: Bob Kane, Jerry Robinson, George Roussos

FEBRUARY 1941; NO. 48

Cover artists: Bob Kane, Jerry Robinson, George Roussos

MARCH 1941; NO. 49
Cover artists: Bob Kane, Jerry Robinson

APRIL 1941; NO. 50
Cover artists: Bob Kane, Jerry Robinson

MAY 1941; NO. 51
Cover artists: Bob Kane, Jerry Robinson

JUNE 1941; NO. 52

Cover artists: Bob Kane, Jerry Robinson

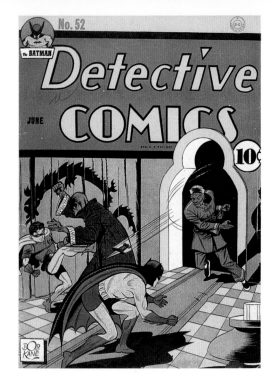

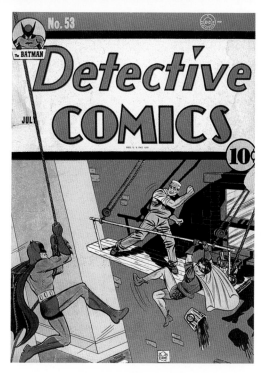

JULY 1941; NO. 53
Cover artists: Bob Kane, Jerry Robinson

AUGUST 1941; NO. 54

Cover artists: Bob Kane, Jerry Robinson, George Roussos

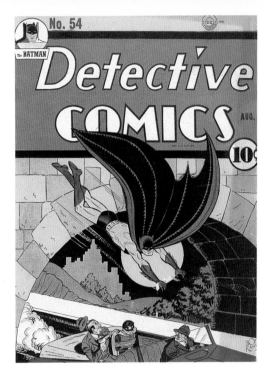

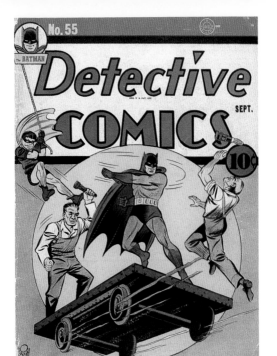

SEPTEMBER 1941; NO. 55
Cover artists: Bob Kane, Jerry Robinson

OCTOBER 1941; NO. 56
Cover artists: Bob Kane, Jerry Robinson

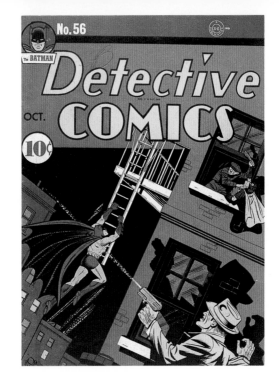

NOVEMBER 1941; NO. 57
Cover artists: Bob Kane, Jerry Robinson, George Roussos

DECEMBER 1941; NO. 58
Cover artists: Fred Ray, Jerry Robinson

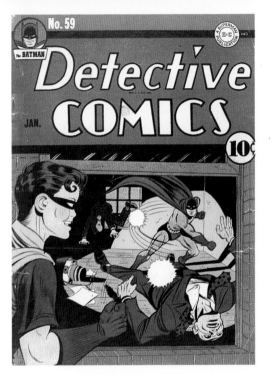

JANUARY 1942; NO. 59
Cover artists: Bob Kane, Jerry Robinson, George Roussos

MARCH 1942; NO. 61

Cover artists: Bob Kane, Jerry Robinson, George Roussos

APRIL 1942; NO. 62
Cover artist: Jerry Robinson

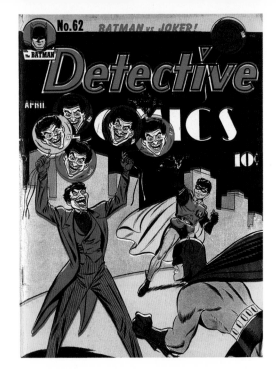

MAY 1942; NO. 63
Cover artists: Fred Ray, Jerry Robinson

JUNE 1942; NO. 64
Cover artist: Jerry Robinson

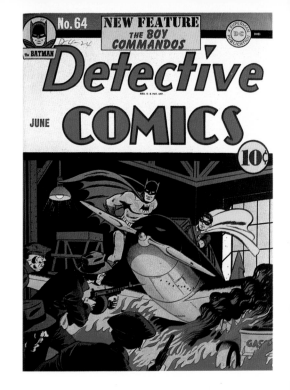

JULY 1942; NO. 65
Cover artists: Jack Kirby, Joe Simon, Jerry Robinson

AUGUST 1942; NO. 66
Cover artists: Jerry Robinson, George Roussos

SEPTEMBER 1942; NO. 67
Cover artist: Jerry Robinson

NOVEMBER 1942; NO. 69

Cover artist: Jerry Robinson

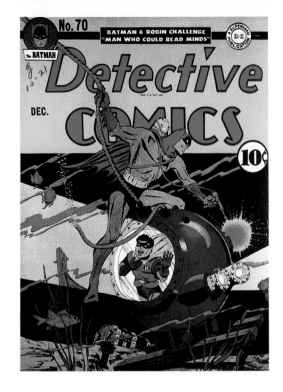

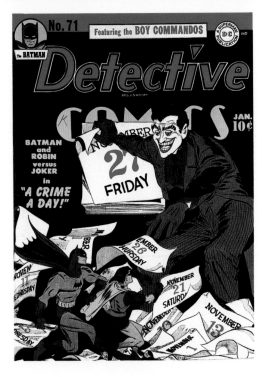

JANUARY 1943; NO. 71

Cover artist: Jerry Robinson

MARCH 1943; NO. 73
Cover artists: Bob Kane, Jerry Robinson

MAY 1943; NO. 75
Cover artists: Bob Kane, George Roussos

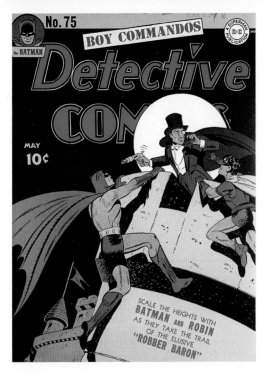

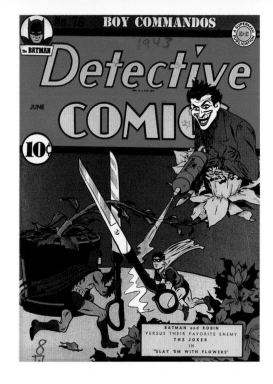

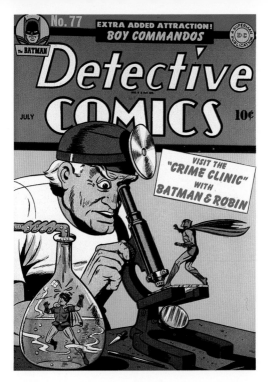

JULY 1943; NO. 77
Cover artists: Bob Kane, George Roussos

AUGUST 1943; NO. 78

Cover artists: Jack Burnley, George Roussos, Jerry Robinson

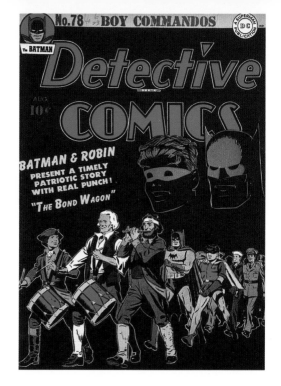

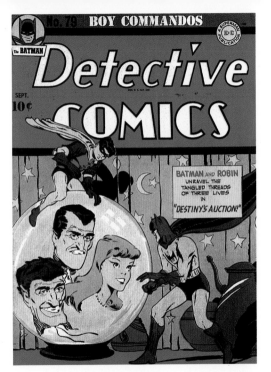

SEPTEMBER 1943; NO. 79
Cover artist: Jerry Robinson

OCTOBER 1943; NO. 80

Cover artists: Bob Kane, Jerry Robinson, George Roussos

NOVEMBER 1943; NO. 81
Cover artists: Bob Kane, Jerry Robinson, George Roussos

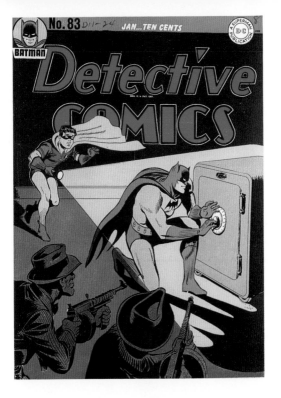

JANUARY 1944; NO. 83
Cover artist: Jack Burnley

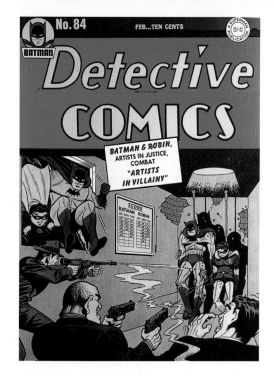

MARCH 1944; NO. 85
Cover artist: Dick Sprang

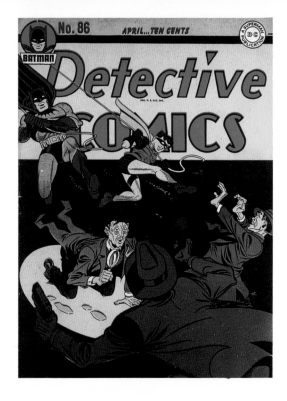

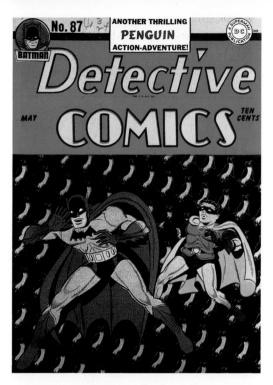

MAY 1944; NO. 87
Cover artist: Dick Sprang

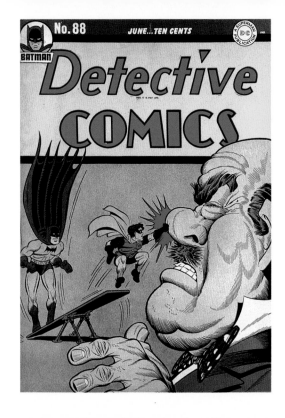

JULY 1944; NO. 89
Cover artist: Dick Sprang

AUGUST 1944; NO. 90
Cover artist: Dick Sprang

SEPTEMBER 1944; NO. 91
Cover artist: Dick Sprang

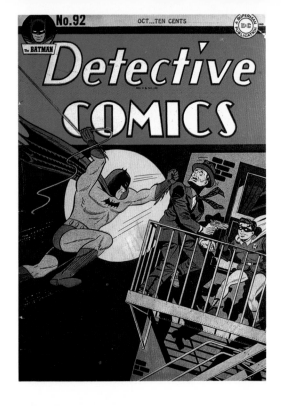

NOVEMBER 1944; NO. 93
Cover artist: Dick Sprang

DECEMBER 1944; NO. 94
Cover artist: Jerry Robinson

JANUARY 1945; NO. 95
Cover artists: Bob Kane, George Roussos

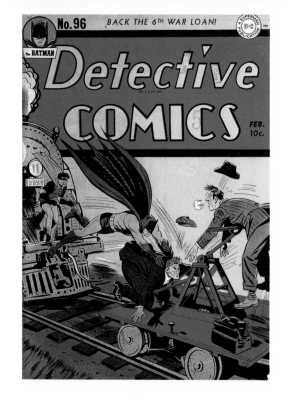

MARCH 1945; NO. 97
Cover artist: Dick Sprang

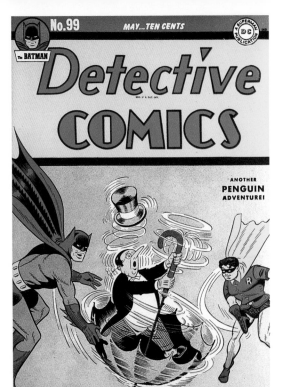

MAY 1945; NO. 99
Cover artist: Dick Sprang

JUNE 1945; NO. 100
Cover artist: Dick Sprang

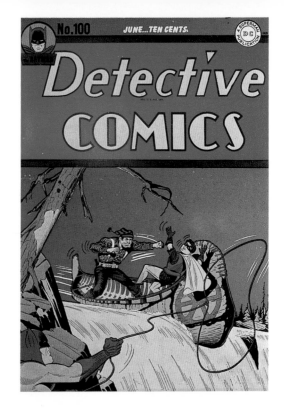

AUGUST 1945; NO. 102
Cover artist: Dick Sprang

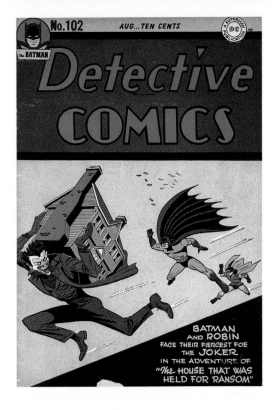

SEPTEMBER 1945; NO. 103

Cover artist: Dick Sprang

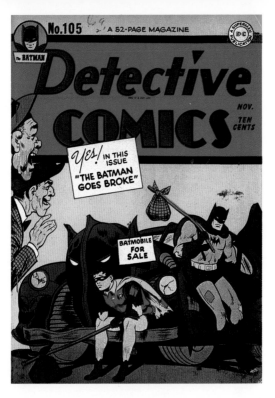

NOVEMBER 1945; NO. 105
Cover artist: Jack Burnley; Charles Paris

DECEMBER 1945; NO. 106
Cover artist: Dick Sprang

JANUARY 1946; NO. 107
Cover artist: Dick Sprang

FEBRUARY 1946; NO. 108
Cover artist: George Roussos

MARCH 1946; NO. 109
Cover artist: Jack Burnley, Ray Burnley

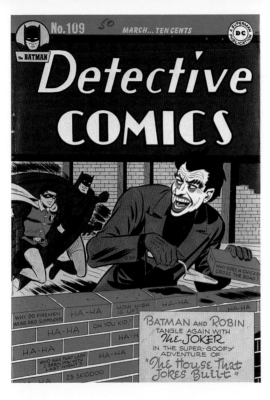

MAY 1946; NO. 111
Cover artist: Win Mortimer

JULY 1946; NO. 113
Cover artist: Dick Sprang

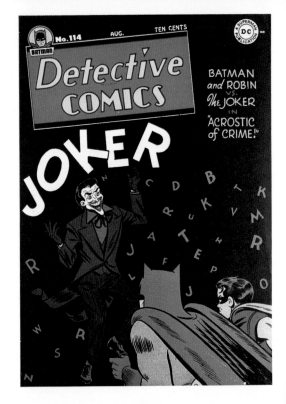

SEPTEMBER 1946; NO. 115
Cover artist: Win Mortimer

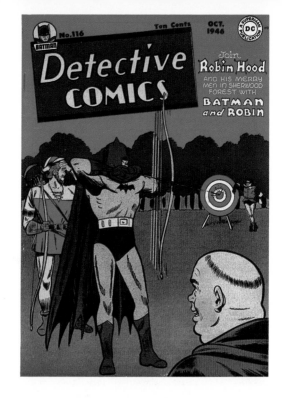

NOVEMBER 1946; NO. 117
Cover artist: Ray Burnley

DECEMBER 1946; NO. 118
Cover artist: Dick Sprang

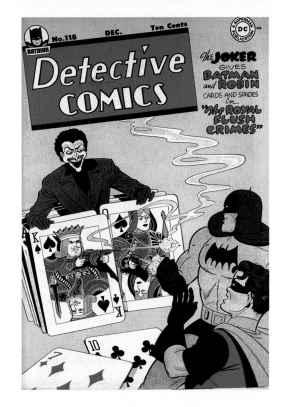

JANUARY 1947; NO. 119
Cover artist: Win Mortimer

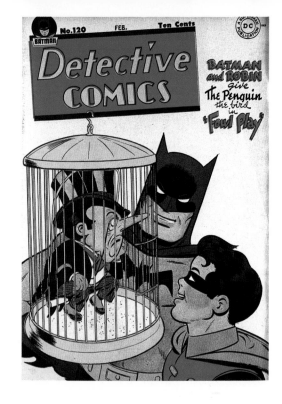

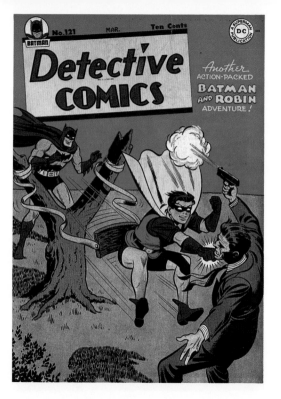

MARCH 1947; NO. 121
Cover artists: Jack Burnley, Charles Paris

MAY 1947; NO. 123
Cover artists: Jack Burnley, Charles Paris

JUNE 1947; NO. 124
Cover artists: Bob Kane, Charles Paris

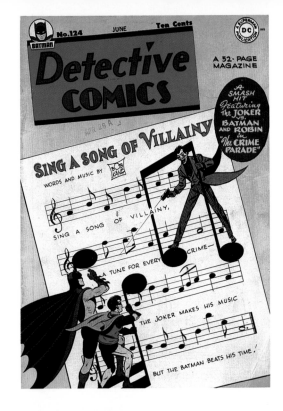

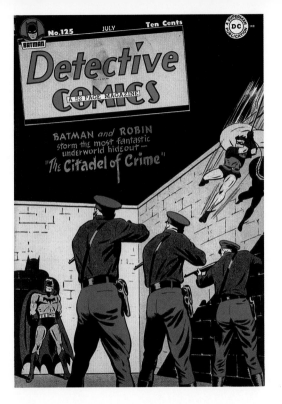

JULY 1947; NO. 125
Cover artists: Jack Burnley, Charles Paris

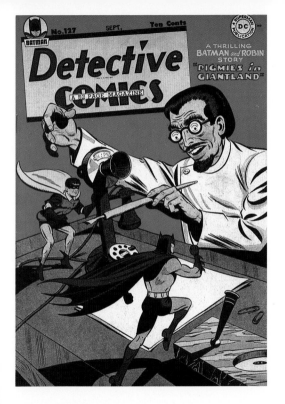

SEPTEMBER 1947; NO. 127
Cover artist: Charles Paris

OCTOBER 1947; NO. 128
Cover artist: Dick Sprang

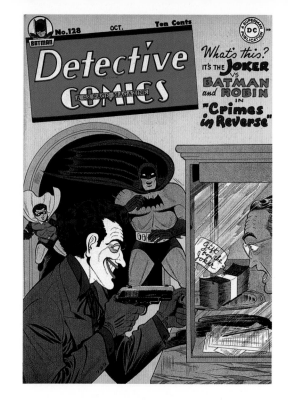

NOVEMBER 1947; NO. 129
Cover artist: Jack Burnley, Charles Paris

JANUARY 1948; NO. 131
Cover artists: Lew Sayre Schwartz, Bob Kane, Charles Paris

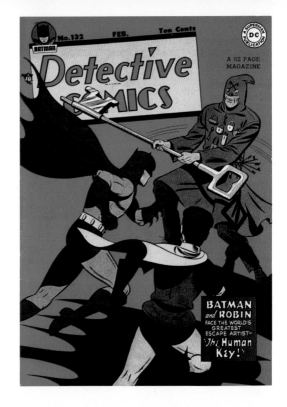

MARCH 1948; NO. 133
Cover artists: Lew Sayre Schwartz, Bob Kane, Charles Paris

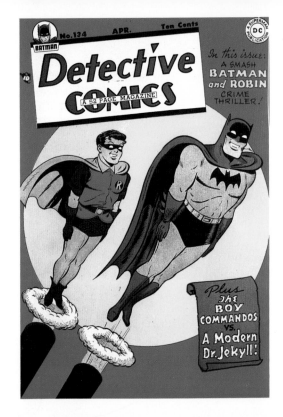

MAY 1948; NO. 135
Cover artists: Lew Sayre Schwartz, Bob Kane, Win Mortimer, Charles Paris

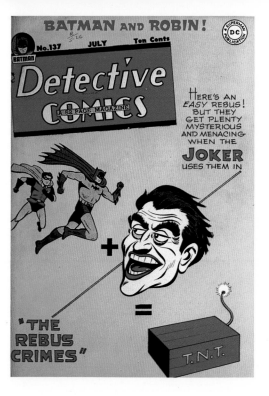

JULY 1948; NO. 137
Cover artists: Bob Kane, Charles Paris

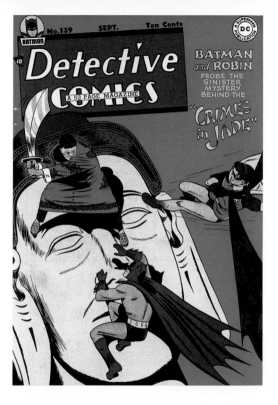

SEPTEMBER 1948; NO. 139
Cover artist: Win Mortimer

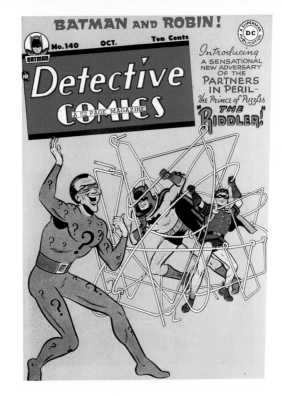

NOVEMBER 1948; NO. 141

Cover artists: Lew Sayre Schwartz, Charles Paris

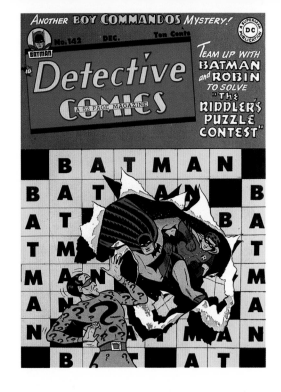

JANUARY 1949; NO. 143

Cover artist: Jim Mooney

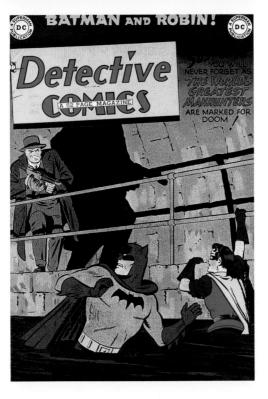

MARCH 1949; NO. 145
Cover artist: Win Mortimer

APRIL 1949; NO. 146
Cover artist: Dick Sprang

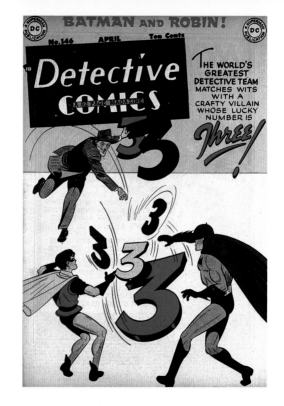

MAY 1949; NO. 147
Cover artist: Dick Sprang

JUNE 1949; NO. 148
Cover artist: Dick Sprang

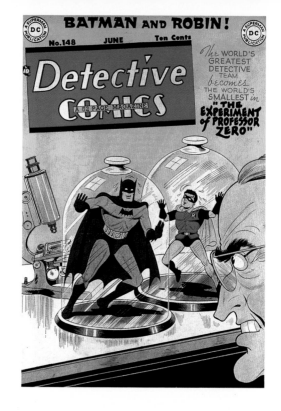

JULY 1949; NO. 149
Cover artist: Dick Sprang

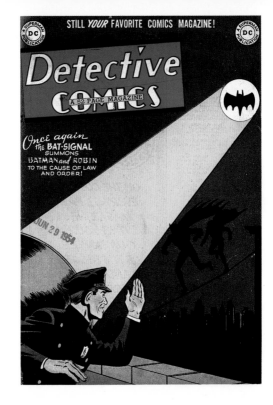

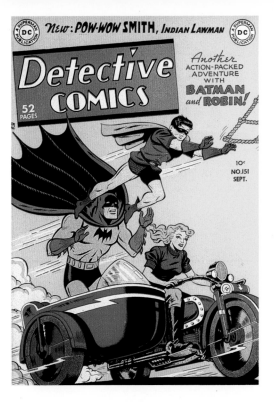

SEPTEMBER 1949; NO. 151
Cover artist: Jim Mooney, Ray Burnley

OCTOBER 1949; NO. 152
Cover artist: Win Mortimer

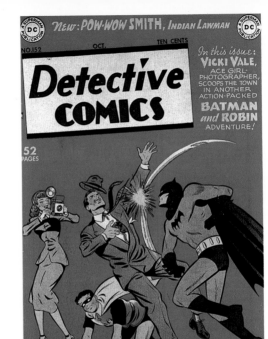

NOVEMBER 1949; NO. 153

Cover artist: Dick Sprang

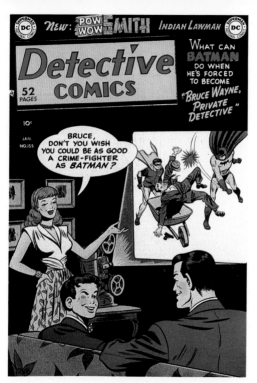

JANUARY 1950; NO. 155

Cover artist: Win Mortimer

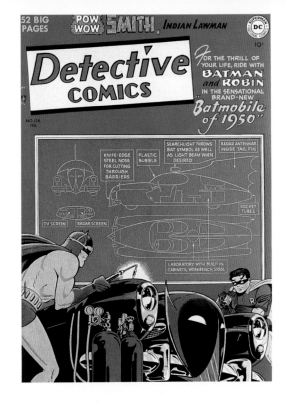

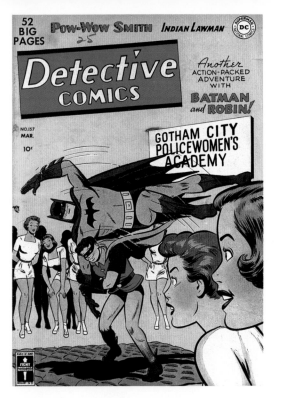

MARCH 1950; NO. 157
Cover artist: Win Mortimer

APRIL 1950; NO. 158
Cover artist: Win Mortimer

MAY 1950; NO. 159
Cover artist: Win Mortimer

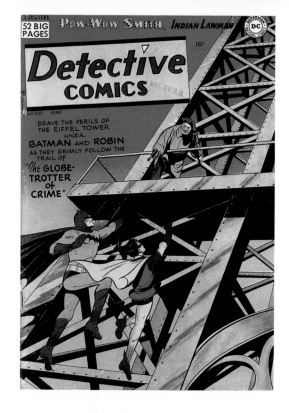

JUNE 1950; NO. 160
Cover artist: Win Mortimer

JULY 1950; NO. 161
Cover artist: Win Mortimer

AUGUST 1950; NO. 162
Cover artist: Win Mortimer

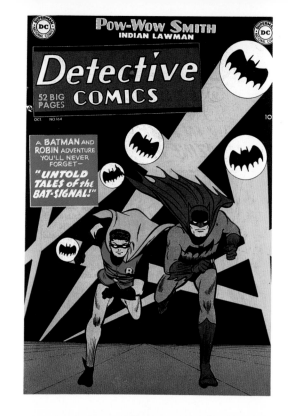

NOVEMBER 1950; NO. 165
Cover artist: Win Mortimer

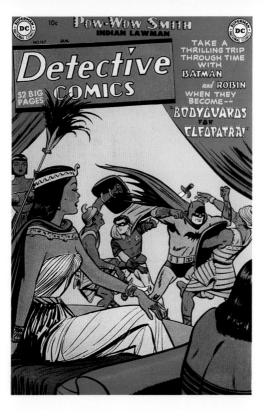

JANUARY 1951; NO. 167
Cover artist: Win Mortimer

FEBRUARY 1951; NO. 168
Cover artists: Lew Sayre Schwartz, Charles Paris

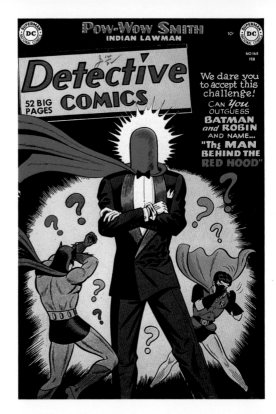

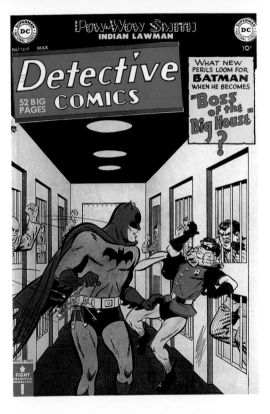

MAY 1951; NO. 171
Cover artist: Win Mortimer

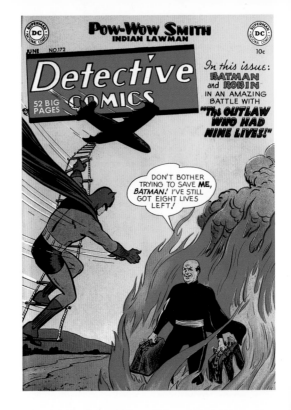

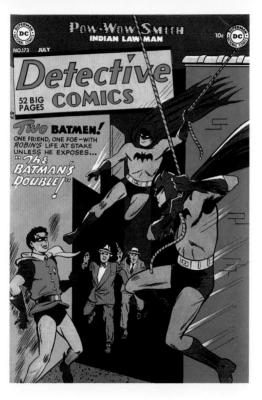

JULY 1951; NO. 173
Cover artist: Win Mortimer

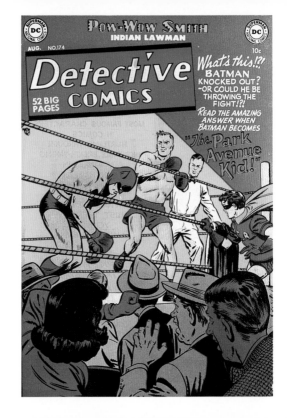

SEPTEMBER 1951; NO. 175
Cover artist: Win Mortimer

NOVEMBER 1951; NO. 177

Cover artist: Win Mortimer

DECEMBER 1951; NO. 178
Cover artist: Win Mortimer

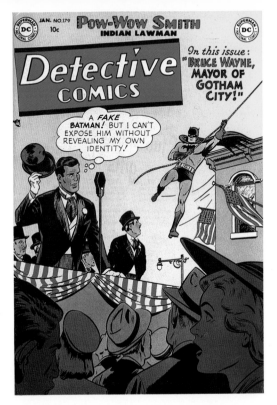

JANUARY 1952; NO. 179

Cover artist: Win Mortimer

FEBRUARY 1952; NO. 180
Cover artist: Win Mortimer

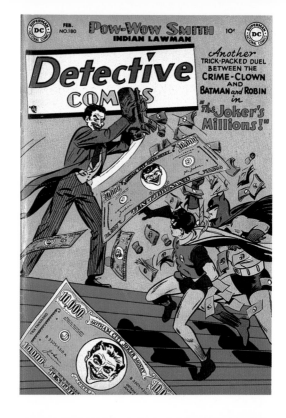

MARCH 1952; NO. 181
Cover artist: Win Mortimer

APRIL 1952; NO. 182
Cover artist: Win Mortimer

MAY 1952; NO. 183
Cover artist: Win Mortimer

JUNE 1952; NO. 184
Cover artist: Win Mortimer

JULY 1952; NO. 185

Cover artist: Win Mortimer

AUGUST 1952; NO. 186
Cover artist: Win Mortimer

OCTOBER 1952; NO. 188
Cover artist: Win Mortimer

NOVEMBER 1952; NO. 189
Cover artist: Win Mortimer

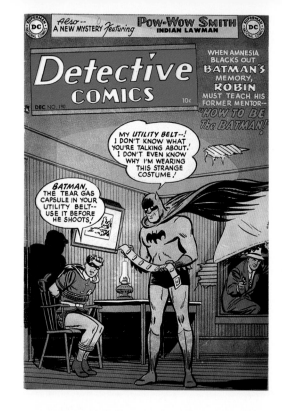

JANUARY 1953; NO. 191

Cover artist: Win Mortimer

FEBRUARY 1953; NO. 192
Cover artist: Win Mortimer

MARCH 1953; NO. 193
Cover artist: Win Mortimer

MAY 1953; NO. 195
Cover artist: Win Mortimer

JULY 1953; NO. 197
Cover artist: Win Mortimer

SEPTEMBER 1953; NO. 199
Cover artist: Win Mortimer

NOVEMBER 1953; NO. 201
Cover artist: Win Mortimer

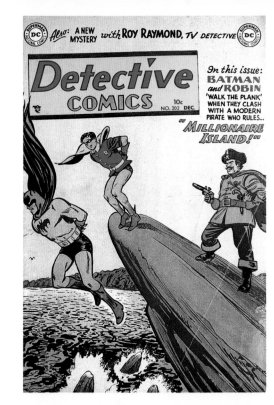

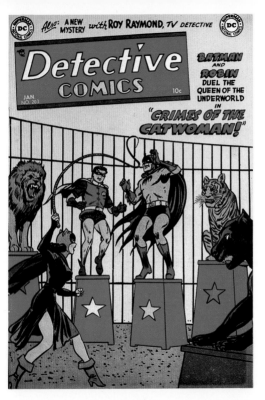

JANUARY 1954; NO. 203
Cover artist: Win Mortimer

FEBRUARY 1954; NO. 204
Cover artist: Win Mortimer

MARCH 1954; NO. 205
Cover artist: Win Mortimer

MAY 1954; NO. 207
Cover artist: Win Mortimer

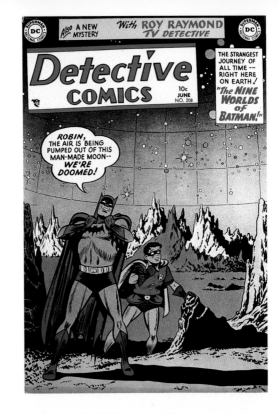

JULY 1954; NO. 209
Cover artist: Win Mortimer

AUGUST 1954; NO. 210
Cover artist: Win Mortimer

SEPTEMBER 1954; NO. 211
Cover artist: Win Mortimer

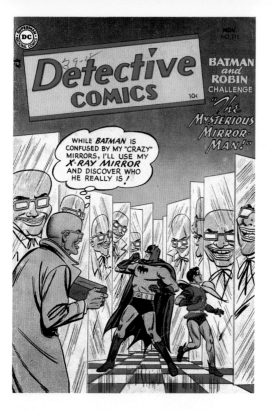

NOVEMBER 1954; NO. 213
Cover artist: Win Mortimer

DECEMBER 1954; NO. 214
Cover artist: Win Mortimer

JANUARY 1955; NO. 215

Cover artists: Sheldon Moldoff, Charles Paris

FEBRUARY 1955; NO. 216

Cover artist: Win Mortimer

APRIL 1955; NO. 218
Cover artist: Win Mortimer

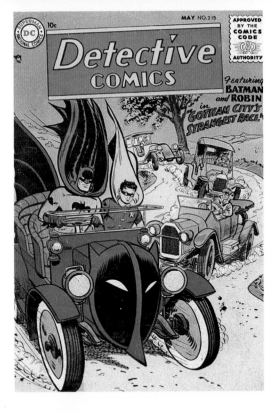

MAY 1955; NO. 219
Cover artist: Win Mortimer

JULY 1955; NO. 221
Cover artist: Win Mortimer

SEPTEMBER 1955; NO. 223

Cover artist: Win Mortimer

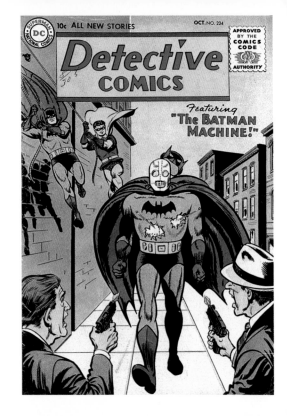

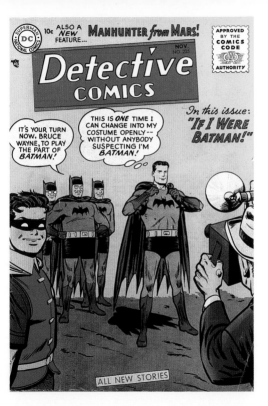

NOVEMBER 1955; NO. 225
Cover artist: Win Mortimer

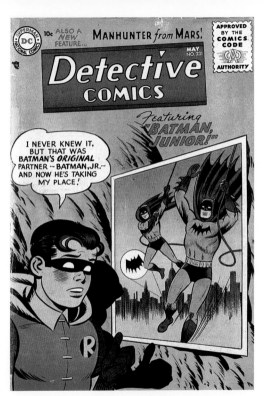

MAY 1956; NO. 231
Cover artists: Sheldon Moldoff, Stan Kaye

JULY 1956; NO. 233
Cover artist: Sheldon Moldoff

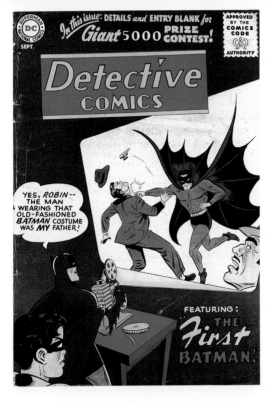

NOVEMBER 1956; NO. 237
Cover artist: Sheldon Moldoff

JANUARY 1957; NO. 239
Cover artists: Sheldon Moldoff, Jack Adler

MARCH 1957; NO. 241
Cover artist: Sheldon Moldoff

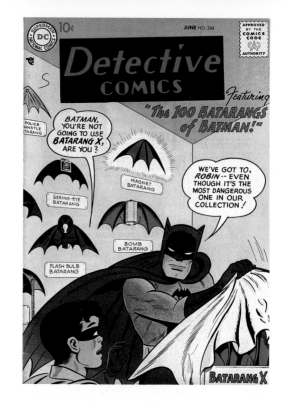

JULY 1957; NO. 245
Cover artist: Sheldon Moldoff

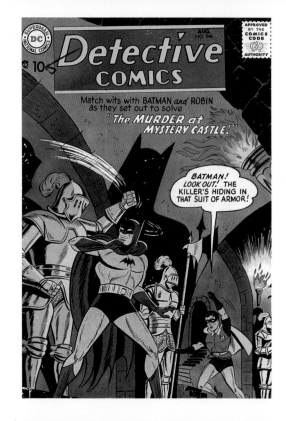

SEPTEMBER 1957; NO. 247
Cover artists: Curt Swan, Stan Kaye

NOVEMBER 1957; NO. 249
Cover artist: Sheldon Moldoff

JANUARY 1958; NO. 251
Cover artist: Sheldon Moldoff

MARCH 1958; NO. 253
Cover artist: Sheldon Moldoff

APRIL 1958; NO. 254
Cover artist: Sheldon Moldoff

MAY 1958; NO. 255
Cover artist: Sheldon Moldoff

JULY 1958; NO. 257
Cover artists: Curt Swan, Stan Kaye

SEPTEMBER 1958; NO. 259
Cover artists: Curt Swan, Stan Kaye

JANUARY 1959; NO. 263
Cover artists: Curt Swan, Stan Kaye

MARCH 1959; NO. 265
Cover artists: Curt Swan, Stan Kaye

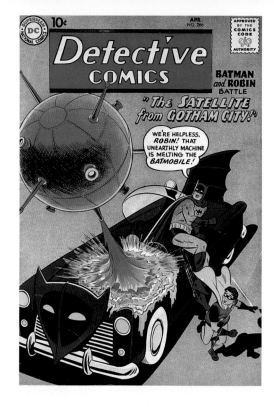

MAY 1959; NO. 267
Cover artists: Curt Swan, Stan Kaye

JUNE 1959; NO. 268
Cover artists: Curt Swan, Stan Kaye

JULY 1959; NO. 269
Cover artists: Curt Swan, Stan Kaye

AUGUST 1959; NO. 270
Cover artists: Curt Swan, Stan Kaye

SEPTEMBER 1959; NO. 271
Cover artists: Curt Swan, Stan Kaye

OCTOBER 1959; NO. 272
Cover artists: Curt Swan, Stan Kaye

NOVEMBER 1959; NO. 273
Cover artist: Sheldon Moldoff

DECEMBER 1959; NO. 274
Cover artist: Sheldon Moldoff

JANUARY 1960; NO. 275
Cover artist: Sheldon Moldoff

MAY 1960; NO. 279
Cover artist: Sheldon Moldoff

JULY 1960; NO. 281
Cover artist: Sheldon Moldoff

NOVEMBER 1960; NO. 285
Cover artist: Sheldon Moldoff

JANUARY 1961: NO. 287
Cover artist: Sheldon Moldoff

MARCH 1961; NO. 289
Cover artist: Sheldon Moldoff

MAY 1961; NO. 291
Cover artist: Sheldon Moldoff

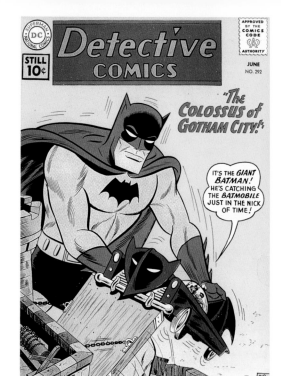

JULY 1961; NO. 293
Cover artist: Sheldon Moldoff

SEPTEMBER 1961; NO. 295

Cover artist: Sheldon Moldoff

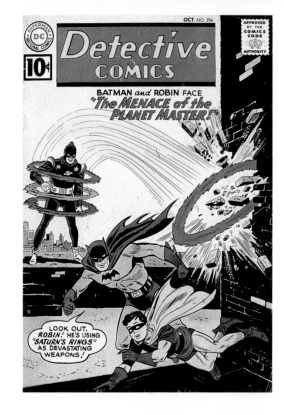

NOVEMBER 1961; NO. 297
Cover artist: Sheldon Moldoff